The Best Places

Written by Robin Bloksberg

Illustrated by Jane Caminos

The best place for a red robin is in its nest.

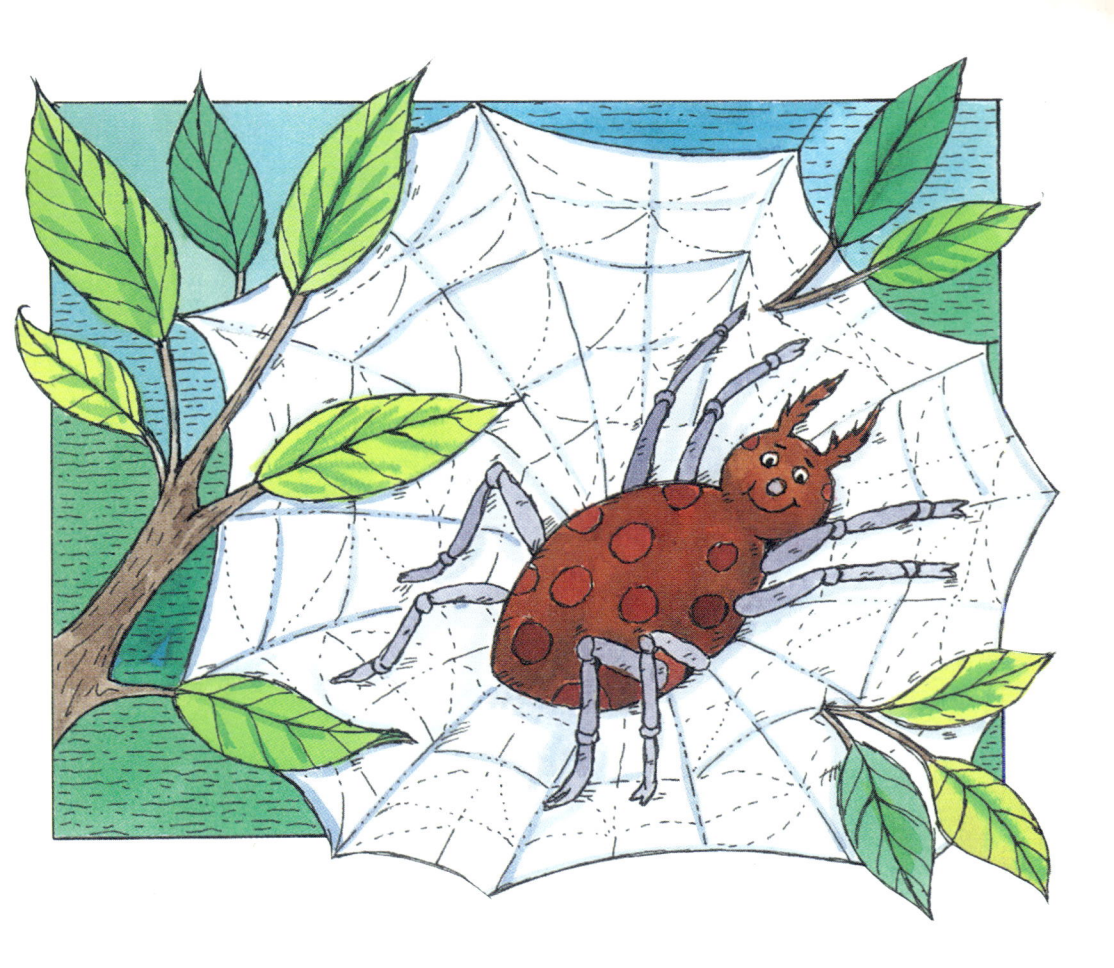

The best place for a spider is in its web.

The best place for a sled is in the snow.

The best place for wet boots is on the mat.

The best place for my pet is on my lap.

The best place for rest is in my bed.

And this is the best place to stop!